# Mysterious Crop
# CIRCLES

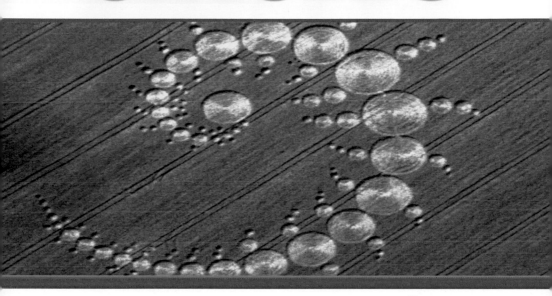

**Rob Waring,** *Series Editor*

T0052350

HEINLE
CENGAGE Learning

Australia • Brazil • Japan • Korea • Mexico • Singapore • Spain • United Kingdom • United States

# Words to Know

This story is set in the United Kingdom. It takes place in the southern part of England.

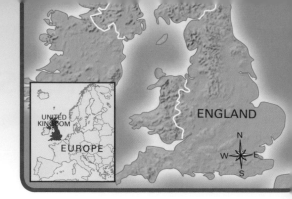

 **Crop Circles.** Read the paragraph. Then match each word or phrase with the correct definition.

Crop circles are large areas of flattened wheat or corn that mysteriously appear in fields of crops. This strange phenomenon has been found all over the world. Several of these unusual circles have even appeared in the landscapes of southern England. Many crop circle researchers say that the circles are created by people, but others believe that aliens make the formations. These people say that the circles are formed when strange beings come to Earth from outer space in their UFOs!

| | |
|---|---|
| **1.** crops _____ | **a.** plants grown by farmers for food |
| **2.** phenomenon _____ | **b.** a living being from a planet other than Earth |
| **3.** landscape _____ | **c.** the area where other planets and the stars are |
| **4.** alien _____ | **d.** an unusual occurrence or happening |
| **5.** outer space _____ | **e.** an area of countryside |
| **6.** UFO _____ | **f.** an unidentified flying object often thought to be from another planet |

**A Crop Circle in a Field of Wheat**

**B** **Other Mysterious Signs.** Read the paragraph and notice the words in **bold**. Then answer the questions.

   Some people believe crop circles are messages from **extraterrestrials**. However, in the past, people on Earth have made some other interesting **signs** as well. In the English countryside, you can see **enormous** stones that are set carefully in circles, like the famous Stonehenge. You can also see amazing animal shapes that were **carved** out of hillsides long ago, such as the White Horses in the south of England.

**1.** Where do extraterrestrials come from? _____

**2.** What does the word 'sign' mean in this context? _____

**3.** What is another word for 'enormous'? _____

**4.** What is the definition of the verb 'carve'? _____

Stonehenge

A White Horse Carving on an English Hillside

Since the beginning of their existence, human beings have created signs on the landscapes in which they live. People from many cultures have long built unusual constructions, including different types of stone circles. In some places they have also carved animals, such as horses, into the hillsides. No one really knows why ancient civilizations originally made these structures and carvings. Some people suggest that different cultures may have constructed them as ways of communicating with aliens. Other people say that the ancient peoples must have created them to please the gods and keep them happy.

The country of England has a very long history, and its landscape has many of these old stone circles and carvings in hillsides. But in recent years, the beautiful rolling countryside of southern England has experienced another unusual phenomenon; one which people all over the world have been studying with great interest. These strange signs have been appearing in local fields and are called 'crop circles.' The strange and mysterious circles are puzzling to everyone, and have many people—even some scientists—asking: who or what could have made them?

 CD 2, Track 07

Did people enter the fields and create these crop circles? Were the circles made by aliens from outer space and sent as messages? The answers to these interesting questions vary and have resulted in a lot of debate among people who are interested in the topic. They have also resulted in a variety of theories about their origins.

Researcher Reg Presley has been investigating crop circles for years. He thinks that most, but not all, crop circles have been created by people. He describes the beginning of his research into the phenomenon some years ago. "I walked into the first crop circle in 1990," he says, "and I thought, 'Hmm … I love puzzles.' And what I did was say, 'Right, I'm going to try and find out what this puzzle's all about.'" And after all of Presley's studies, what is his hypothesis? "I think probably ninety-five percent of them are man-made," he states. But what about the other five percent?

Reg Presley

Presley feels that some of the circles are so huge and complex that it's difficult to comprehend how people could have made them. He says, "There's one [in particular] here, just over on the hill—Milk Hill—it's so enormous, that you can't even see the other side of the crop formation." He then explains that the formation measures over a kilometer* in width. Presley thinks that people couldn't have made such an enormous circle without other people knowing about it. At what time of day could the crop circle makers have created it without being seen? How could they have done it without leaving any evidence? Presley doesn't know, so for him it remains yet another mystery about crop circles.

Presley also points out that these kinds of formations appear not only in England, but all over the world. Similar circles can be found in a number of materials, from wheat, to trees, to ice. However, all of the worldwide appearances share one distinct characteristic: their curious circular shape. Presley tells of a circle that was formed in a forested area near the city of Vancouver, Canada. In this arrangement, the trees were **bent**[1] over and shaped in a circle. It is particularly remarkable due to the fact that, according to Presley, only the top two meters of the trees were bent. The trees were not broken suddenly and quickly as one would expect. Instead, they were bent over—without breaking—and arranged in the same circular spiral manner as the crop circles. Presley has also heard of ice circles, in which a circle of ice is missing from a body of water but the area around it remains frozen. Presley believes that a connection almost certainly exists between all of these mysterious circles.

---

[1]**bent:** not straight; sharply curved

*see page 24 for a metric conversion chart

Unexplained circular shapes have appeared in everything from forest tree tops to ice-covered lakes.

While Presley may have his beliefs about crop circles, others don't think crop circles are really all that mysterious. A young Englishman named Matthew doesn't feel that they are puzzling at all. Matthew is a crop circle maker, and he believes that the circles are always a form of art made by people. In the area near Matthew's home, many crop circles have recently appeared. While he will not admit to making any of these, Matthew has offered to demonstrate exactly how crop circles are made. As he walks near one of the crop circle fields he says, "Yeah, a lot of circles have been appearing in this area." He then talks about how the fields look like blank artistic work space to him; a space that he wants to fill. "It's a lovely landscape," he says, "and the fields are just clean and open like a **canvas**."[2] As he gets his equipment ready for the demonstration, it becomes clear that Matthew is well aware of how crop circles are made.

---

[2] **canvas:** the cloth on which an artist paints

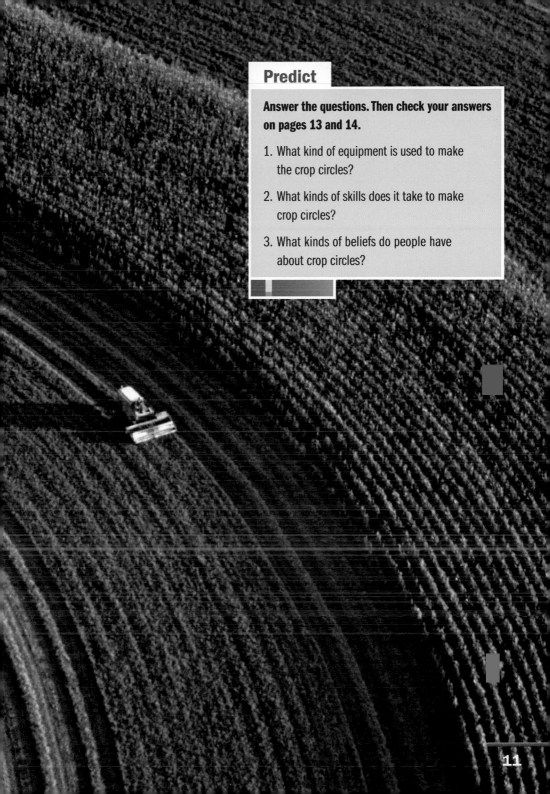

## Predict

**Answer the questions. Then check your answers on pages 13 and 14.**

1. What kind of equipment is used to make the crop circles?

2. What kinds of skills does it take to make crop circles?

3. What kinds of beliefs do people have about crop circles?

Matthew has his own opinions about the alien communication theories as well. He doesn't really believe the idea that the crop circles are aliens' attempts at communicating with Earth. Matthew actually finds the concept a bit amusing. "Well, if there are aliens out there doing it," he smiles, "they're using **stomper boards**[3] and these little markers," he says pointing to the tools in his hand. He then continues to explain why he feels this way, "Because there [are] things there like **combing effects**[4], which are people going around and around and around the same area, flattening it down." Matthew then adds, "That wouldn't be there with aliens I'm sure."

In fact, Matthew thinks aliens would more likely use a faster, **instantaneous**[5] technique. He also thinks this kind of mysterious 'alien method' would be something that was obviously real to everyone—even him. Unfortunately for those who believe in crop circles, this kind of evidence is something that Matthew has never seen. The only crop circles that he has seen were undoubtedly made by human beings—and moreover, he knows how they were made.

---

[3]**stomper boards:** wooden boards that crop circle makers use to flatten fields
[4]**combing effects:** the appearance that a crop has been laid down and shaped, as if styled with a hair comb
[5]**instantaneous:** something which happens instantly; immediate

As Matthew and his team begin the long evening task of making a crop circle, Matthew talks about some of the beliefs regarding them. He explains that some people imagine seeing extraterrestrials, strange balls of light, or UFOs when they see a crop circle. Matthew, however, claims that crop circle design is actually a creative art form that is done by human artists. He and his team of two other young men have come to the field to show how it is done. They begin by walking around and around in various sectors of the field. As they go, they use their stomper boards to flatten the **grain**[6] into large shapes and patterns. It takes a long time, and a lot of labor is required. As time passes and one sees the crop circle slowly take form, it's easy to see that man-made crop circles are completely possible.

---

[6]**grain:** a long-stemmed food product used to make breads and cereals

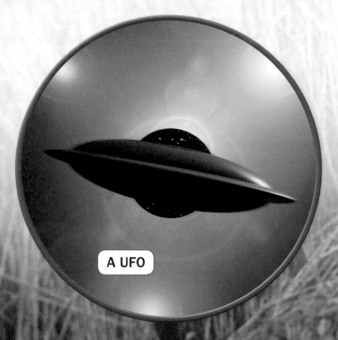

A UFO

Matthew then explains that crop circle design and creation often become a kind of competition. Teams of artists and designers sometimes challenge each other to see who can come up with the best designs. An enormous crop circle can have a huge impact on people. The designers also want to impress and amaze the public by showing what they can complete in an evening. That's the challenge of crop circle design, and that's also why it is so interesting and appealing to the designers.

Timing, however, is one of the biggest challenges for these crop circle artists. Designing and then making crop circles without being seen is very difficult; but, it's not impossible—and it's certainly not a mystery. Matthew explains how it's done. The basic principle is that teams have to work very quickly and efficiently. They must do so in order to avoid being caught and getting into trouble with the authorities. As Matthew describes the process, it's obvious that it's exciting for him. "It is a bit like a **military**[7] operation," he explains. "You've got to get in, do the job, get out, [and] not get caught, you know?" He then adds, "It's **SAS**,[8] I suppose. **'Who dares wins'**."[9]

---

[7]**military:** of or related to the armed forces of a country
[8]**SAS:** a part of the British Army called Special Air Services (SAS)
[9]**"Who dares wins":** an SAS saying that means you must be fearless to win

Excitement aside, Matthew does have some concerns about the crop circle phenomenon, but they're not about the people making them. Matthew is concerned about some of the people who think the alien theories are true. "I'm a little bit worried about some of the beliefs I hear going around," he reports. A wide range of theories are occasionally discussed in the media; some of them almost seem to have a religious element to them or even relate to the end of the world. "Some of the stuff is a bit **apocalyptic**,"[10] Matthew reports. Another disturbing aspect is that some people try to influence others about crop circles and what they represent. They try to get other people to believe in, or follow, some very unusual theories.

These strange beliefs don't fool Matthew, of course. He has been researching, as well as designing and making, crop circles for a number of years. In all of that time, he insists that he's never seen any confirmation that aliens are making these mysterious, unexplained circles in the fields. He feels that the crop circles show signs of creative human beings, not extraterrestrials. In his opinion, crop circles are definitely not signs of intelligent life in outer space. However in some people's minds, opinions like Matthew's might be a sign of another kind of intelligent life—intelligent life on Earth!

---

[10]**apocalyptic:** about the end of the world

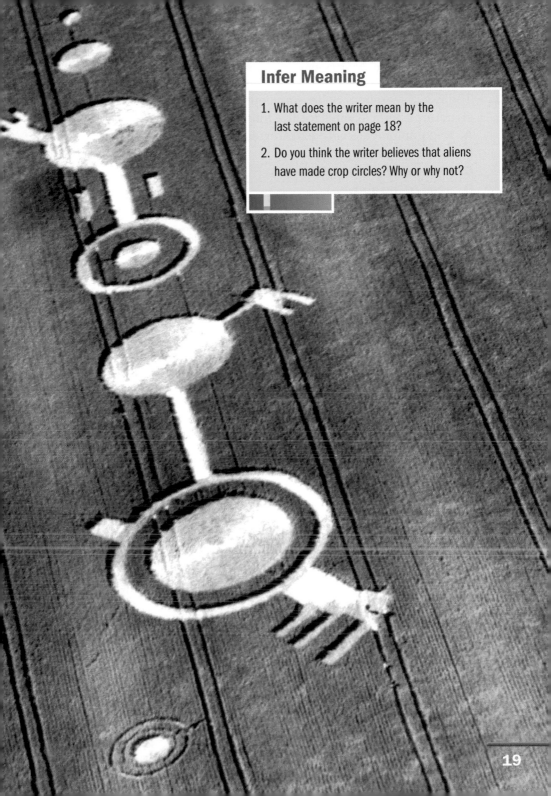

### Infer Meaning

1. What does the writer mean by the last statement on page 18?

2. Do you think the writer believes that aliens have made crop circles? Why or why not?

# After You Read

1.  Today's researchers believe ancient peoples may have created structures and carvings for the following reasons EXCEPT:
    A. to communicate with extraterrestrials
    B. for religious purposes
    C. to show respect for horses
    D. none of the above

2.  When Reg Presley says he loves puzzles, what does he mean?
    A. He wants to solve the crop circle mystery.
    B. He loves to play games.
    C. He doesn't know the answer.
    D. He thinks crop circles are difficult.

3.  Reg Presley suggests that crop circles are created by:
    A. people
    B. aliens
    C. both people and aliens
    D. unknown

4.  On page 10, what does the writer NOT suggest about Matthew?
    A. He likes crop circles.
    B. He thinks aliens make crop circles.
    C. He is an artist.
    D. He disagrees with Presley.

5.  In paragraph 1 on page 13, in the phrase 'flattening it down,' 'it' refers to:
    A. the stomper board
    B. the field
    C. the marker
    D. a UFO

6.  In paragraph 2 on page 13, the word 'undoubtedly' is closest in meaning to:
    A. imposing
    B. without question
    C. uncertainly
    D. consequently

**7.** On page 14, when Matthew uses the phrase 'imagine seeing' this suggests that he believes people:

  **A.** actually see aliens
  **B.** pretend to see aliens
  **C.** see evidence of aliens
  **D.** perceive that they see aliens

**8.** According to Matthew, why do artists create crop circles?

  **A.** to impress people
  **B.** to make puzzles for artists
  **C.** to trick other artists
  **D.** to show that artists can have fun

**9.** What do the letters SAS stand for?

  **A.** Special Airforce Services
  **B.** Special Alien Services
  **C.** Special Air Searches
  **D.** Special Air Services

**10.** According to Matthew, why is making crop circles like a military operation?

  **A.** because it's serious
  **B.** because it's dangerous
  **C.** because it's secretive
  **D.** because it's apocalyptic

**11.** Matthew has never seen _____ that proves aliens make crop circles.

  **A.** many things
  **B.** nothing
  **C.** everything
  **D.** anything

**12.** The writer probably thinks that Matthew is:

  **A.** an ordinary man
  **B.** wrong about crop circles
  **C.** right about crop circles
  **D.** a liar

# HEINLE Times

# CROP CIRCLES: FACT OR FICTION?

The Heinle Times recently published an article about crop circles which brought interesting and varied responses from several readers. Here are two of these letters:

## More info, please!

Your recent article on crop circles failed to include several important points. First of all, there was no mention of the huge volume of sightings over the past 50 years. According to one source, there have been over 10,000 documented reports of crop circles, as well as several other unofficial ones. You also failed to include statistics showing how widespread this phenomenon is. Crop circles have been documented in more than 29 countries—and that's just in the official reports!

In addition, observers at crop circle sites have noted that many of the plants are broken several inches above the ground, but the lower parts are not damaged. This simply wouldn't happen if people were using stomper boards. Also, soil taken from the inside of some crop circles indicates that it has been heated—possibly to as high as 1500° Celsius. I believe we need to take these findings—and their statistics—seriously if we are going to find out the truth about this amazing phenomenon.

Yours truly,
Richard Wellner

# You've got to be kidding!

Your recent article on crop circles incorrectly gave the impression that crop circles are a valid scientific phenomenon! I think that this is a serious error in judgment on the part of this newspaper. Most people in the scientific community agree that crop circles are the work of humans who enjoy playing jokes on other people. They are not the result of visits by extraterrestrial beings!

Three years ago your newspaper featured an article about David Chorley and Douglas Bower. These two painters, who live in the English countryside, explained that they have been making crop circles together for years. They claim to be responsible for as many as 25 to 30 of them annually. I also recently discovered a Web site that describes exactly how to make crop circles. It has links with headings like 'tools' and 'techniques.' I feel that a responsible newspaper like the Heinle Times should not support the belief that aliens are responsible for crop circles.

Sincerely,
Dr. Ralph Aker, Ph D.
Boston University

"Most people in the scientific community agree that crop circles are the work of humans who enjoy playing jokes on other people."

CD 2, Track 08

Word Count: 369
Time: _____

# Vocabulary List

**alien** (2, 4, 7, 13, 18, 19)
**apocalyptic** (18)
**bent** (8)
**canvas** (10)
**carve** (3, 4)
**combing effect** (13)
**crop** (2, 3, 4, 7, 8, 10, 11, 13, 14, 17, 18, 19)
**enormous** (3, 8, 17)
**extraterrestrial** (3, 14, 18)
**grain** (14)
**instantaneous** (13)
**landscape** (2, 4, 10)
**military** (17)
**outer space** (2, 7, 18)
**phenomenon** (2, 4, 7, 18)
**SAS** (17)
**sign** (3, 4, 18)
**stomper board** (13, 14)
**UFO** (2, 14)
**who dares wins** (17)

## Metric Conversion Chart

**Area**
1 hectare = 2.471 acres

**Length**
1 centimeter = .394 inches
1 meter = 1.094 yards
1 kilometer = .621 miles

**Temperature**
0° Celsius = 32° Fahrenheit

**Volume**
1 liter = 1.057 quarts

**Weight**
1 gram = .035 ounces
1 kilogram = 2.2 pounds